MW00781691

The Prairie Dog

by Betsy Samuels

SCHOOL PUBLISHERS

Cover ©Photodisc; 3 ©Photodisc; 4 (t) ©Corbis Royalty Free; (b) ©Harcourt Education/Lewis Chandler; 5–6 ©Photolibrary.com; 7 ©Harcourt Education/Lewis Chandler; 8 ©Getty Images; 9 ©Photolibrary.com/Animals Animals; 10–11 ©Photolibrary.com; 12 ©Photodisc; 13 ©Photolibrary.com; 14 ©Photodisc

Printed in Mexico

ISBN 10: 10: 0-15-351431-0
ISBN 13: 978-0-15-351431-9

Ordering Options
ISBN 10: 0-15-351212-1 (Grade 2 Advanced-Level Collection)
ISBN 13: 978-0-15-351212-4 (Grade 2 Advanced-Level Collection)
ISBN 10: 0-15-358066-6 (package of 5)
ISBN 13: 978-0-15-358066-6 (package of 5)

2 3 4 5 6 7 8 9 10   050   15 14 13 12 11 10 09 08 07

Prairie Dog Town

Down this tunnel is a prairie dog burrow. Prairie dogs live together in towns. A town is a large network of tunnels under the ground.

Prairie dogs live here.

Prairie Dogs?

Prairie dogs are not true dogs at all. They belong to the squirrel family. They are about the size of a rabbit.

Prairie dogs live in some of the western parts of North America.

Family Groups

Many family groups of prairie dogs live in a town. These groups are called coteries. Most coteries have one adult male, some adult females, and their young. Each coterie lives in its own burrow.

Burrows

Prairie dogs use their sharp claws to dig burrows. They kick the dirt out with their back legs. The dirt makes a mound at the entrance of the burrow. The dirt mound helps to keep the burrow from flooding.

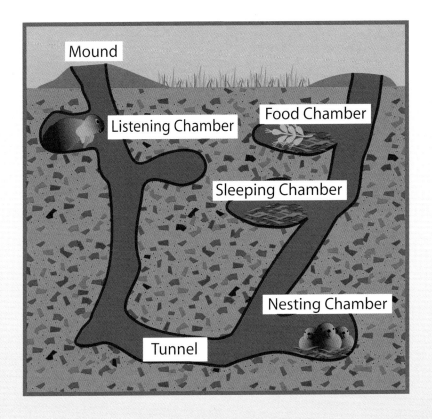

Mound

Listening Chamber

Food Chamber

Sleeping Chamber

Nesting Chamber

Tunnel

Inside the Burrow

There are many chambers and tunnels inside the burrow. Chambers near the top of the burrow are used for listening for danger. There are also chambers suitable for storing food, for nesting, and for sleeping. Some chambers are used for escaping from predators.

Working Together

Prairie dogs in a coterie groom each other, play together, and raise their young. They also work together to defend their territory from predators, such as badgers, coyotes, and eagles.

Raising the Young

Prairie dogs mate once a year. About
one month later, a litter of pups is born in
the burrow. The newborn pups have no fur
and their eyes are sealed shut. They start
to get fur at about three weeks. When they
are about five weeks old, their eyes open.

While they are in the burrow, the mother feeds and grooms the pups. They go outside the burrow when they are about six weeks old. They feed on milk from their mother for about seven weeks. Then they start to eat solid food.

Leaving the Nest

A female prairie dog usually remains in the same coterie her whole life. Males disappear from the coterie when they are about one year old. They usually join a nearby coterie.

Defending the Territory

Prairie dogs "kiss" one another by touching their front teeth together. This is how they identify whether another prairie dog is part of their coterie. They will attack prairie dogs that are not part of their coterie.

Prairie dogs look out for predators. They stand on the dirt mound of their burrow. If they see danger, they make a barking sound. Other members of the town hear the barking, and they also let out warning barks. This barking pattern warns all the members of a town that a predator is near.

Living Together

Prairie dogs are social animals. They crowd together on their dirt mounds. They lay in the sun together. They carefully groom one another. They sleep together at night in their burrows. Prairie dogs work together to look after one another and keep their towns safe.

Think Critically

1. What does the text mean when it says that prairie dogs are "social animals"?

2. What are the stages that a baby prairie dog goes through during its first seven weeks of life?

3. How is a whole town of prairie dogs warned about a danger?

4. What can you learn by looking at the diagram on page 7?

5. What did you find most surprising about prairie dogs?

 Science

Make a Venn Diagram Make a Venn diagram comparing a dog to a prairie dog. Draw a picture of a prairie dog.

School-Home Connection Read *The Prairie Dog* to a family member. Talk about the differences between prairie dogs and pet dogs.

Word Count: 492 (507 with words in graphics)